Come Fly with Me
through the
Gift of Words

Come Fly with Me

through the

Gift of Words

WENDY BROOKS

iUniverse

COME FLY WITH ME THROUGH THE GIFT OF WORDS

iUniverse books may be ordered through booksellers or by contacting:

iUniverse
1663 Liberty Drive
Bloomington, IN 47403
www.iuniverse.com
1-800-Authors (1-800-288-4677)

Because of the dynamic nature of the Internet, any web addresses or links contained in this book may have changed since publication and may no longer be valid. The views expressed in this work are solely those of the author and do not necessarily reflect the views of the publisher, and the publisher hereby disclaims any responsibility for them.

Any people depicted in stock imagery provided by Thinkstock are models, and such images are being used for illustrative purposes only. Certain stock imagery © Thinkstock.

ISBN: 978-1-4917-8196-8 (sc)
ISBN: 978-1-4917-8197-5 (e)

Library of Congress Control Number: 2015919247

Print information available on the last page.

iUniverse rev. date: 11/24/2015

Contents

Acknowledgement

As God loved me, he gave to me my wonderful family. They are the reason my life is so complete. I have been blessed with their love and support, and I thank them with all my heart.

A Black Crow

Above all is the blue sky, ablaze with color, while pillows of white nestle upon the sky.

A black crow flies, its wings spread outward, reaching into that scene.

Its silhouette makes its way across the horizon.

Have we given the crow a wrong image?

Do we think of it only as a scrounger and a scavenger that prowls along the roads?

But do you realize the crow is among the smartest animals on the planet?

They relay messages to their flock and mourn a loss of one of their own.

Do we judge other humans in such a way,

Always believing what is said without analyzing for ourselves,

Observing the outside with no thought as to what may be within?

The next time you see a beautiful crow, give it a wave, and the next time you see a human form, give him a smile.

We are all God's creatures, you see, and we deserve the best this world can provide.

A Day

As we walk through each day of life, we ask our God, What is there for us to do?

What plan is there for us to fill?

What goal is ours to bring about?

How do we show our love for you?

We are ready, willing, waiting, wanting to accomplish—all for you.

But do we realize that each day that we live, we are given the chance:

The chance to meet; the chance to greet;

The chance to calm a troubled heart; the chance to change a life that weeps!

Do we meet that challenge or turn away

Do we think it will happen another day?

A day when we are prepared or feeling okay?

A day when we don't have plans, and it suits our way?

God's way is to be your way.

God's needs are to be your needs.

When God asks, we obey.

So look for the chances—don't run away.

Do God's bidding each and every day,

In small and large ways! Always his way.

Thus you will be God's helper here today.

A Friend

What is a friend?

What does a friend mean to you?

Do we need a friend, and why?

A friend is the person who knows all your secrets, your dreams, your foibles and frailties.

Even in knowing all there is to know about us, friends still honor us with their friendship.

Our friends listen when we need to vent, don't judge us no matter what we say.

Our friends tell us the reality even if it is not our reality,

Giving us the confidence that they will tell us the truth whether or not we want to hear it.

They silently listen so that we might hear and evaluate our own words.

What benefit is that to us?

Inexplicably, one of our most treasured gifts.

The Gift of Friendship.

Giving us the support on decisions to be made.

Giving us the joy of sharing all the blessings in our lives,

Giving us the knowledge that we are cherished by another.

So, do we need a friend?

I would say absolutely, positively, without a doubt we do.

I hope that each and every one who reads this will say,

"I have such a friend."

A Journey

I dreamt last night that I was driving alone.

The direction wasn't right; I knew it in my heart.

But I couldn't stop myself. I couldn't turn back.

I followed the road until I was in destruction.

The buildings were falling; the windows were broken.

The streets were lined with stones and glass.

What had I done? How could I be here?

Had I listened to those who loved me most, or did I go the road I chose without much thought to what was right?

Suddenly the road was clear;

I knew which way I should go.

My eyes popped open; I was in my bed.

A dream it was, but what a dream.

I was given a second chance, a chance to see where I might go if I stayed upon this road.

Thank you, God, for giving me sight and loving me enough to make it right!

A New Life

My life is in shambles.

Situations have been difficult, struggles have continued, directions were unclear, and nothing was as I dreamed it would be.

I wanted to improve the road, clear away the rubble, and stay in the same place.

But the rubble wouldn't move.

Whatever I tried didn't accomplish that which I knew had to be.

Decisions were looming that I didn't want to make; I had a sense of loss, a sense of defeat—not what I was accustomed to.

All my life I have worked hard, dedicated to my goal,

Accomplishing much, but not changing the circumstances that reality showed.

What do I do?

Do I have the courage to change the path?

Do I have the power to change my life, giving up what I have known?

Yes, I will take my life into my hands.

I will move forward, putting behind me that which has been mine.

I will take the good memories, cherish them all; build upon those memories in a new place, a new time.

I will take back the control that is mine.

I will learn the lessons that give me growth.

I will walk the new path that stretches before me.

I will succeed because I know that I can.

I will be victorious because today is the first day of my new life.

A Touch

How do we transfer our feelings?

By speaking our thoughts, by giving another a smile, or by a touch.

The touch of a Mom when she soothes the hurt away.

The touch of a friend as he sees our troubled heart.

The touch of a doctor who mends our broken bodies.

The touch of a spouse who loves us through thick and thin.

The touch of a stranger whom we met today.

The touch of a child who takes our hands and gives us complete trust.

The clasp of hands when we reach out through friendship.

The clasp of a hand when sickness steals our strength.

The touch of God's love when our lives fall apart.

Let our touches be the threads that entwine us together and give us power.

Alone

The people mill around me;

I stand and talk, echoing their laughter.

Yet I feel estranged.

Life's everyday necessities have a new dimension.

Nature's beauty is my refuge, my solace, my peace.

I hunger for the new sky, the flight of a bird, the purity of a flower;

In them, I find a purpose.

The people mill around me.

I listen to their sorrow and feel their pain.

My heart struggles against the complexities of their awareness.

I long to show them eternity!

Not fleeting moments of success, empty vials of wealth, idle moments of pleasure—but lasting peace.

It is there, waiting for all mankind:

Peace for your troubled soul; wealth will not purchase contentment.

Peace for your tormented heart; success will not alleviate your pain.

Peace for your diseased mind; pleasure will not dispel your anguish.

Ask my friend, and peace will be yours.

Perfect peace I wish for you.

Approval

Oh, approval, you smother me with the obligation of your name.

I try to carry the weight and adhere to the necessities, but I feel I fail.

I want to live up to the expectations, but they are like a mountain rising before me.

Is this approval so necessary? Am I making it more difficult than it needs to be?

Am I trying to live up to unrealistic goals?

Am I doing the best I can, truly trying as diligently as possible?

Consider this, then.

If I am, then it is I who am being unrealistic.

I who am asking too much.

I who am not satisfied with my own accomplishments.

Let me reevaluate and give myself approval.

Let me relax and relish where I am.

Let me bask in this newfound approval, enjoy its peace, and then move on.

Beginnings and Endings

Have you pondered the wonder of the soul?

The reason for living for you and me?

Can one small soul perform a miracle?

Can one small soul leave a mark?

Beginnings and endings—they merge into one.

The indelible life, written on the wind, forever to be a part of the universe!

A legacy for all who follow, one small soul joined together with countless more.

The building blocks to knowledge—the knowledge of good!

The choice is ours.

Each soul contributes to the blocks, and thus there are no beginnings or endings.

Bitterness

Bitterness sprays over you like a cold rain,

Chilling you through and through until you feel you will never get warm again.

It saps your strength and allows no light to get into your soul.

People try to cheer you.

People try to encourage you.

People try to make you see reason.

But the more they try, the more you resist.

Why? Why do you resist.

Is the pain so great that you submit?

Can you find the strength to open your heart,

To allow a small ray of light,

To allow a thought of forgiveness?

If you can, it would be a giant step to peace.

For peace cannot enter where bitterness lives;

It is a wall blocking all,

It is the destroyer of your happiness.

Life is too short.

Don't shorten it by your own hand.

Wipe your slate clean and begin again.

Bullying

The act of hurting another person with no provocation!

Hurting not in retaliation for an act perpetuated on us, but for the sole purpose of making life miserable for another!

Have you been the recipient of this kind of treatment?

Have you experienced the sadness when bitter words puncture your soul?

What can you do to prevent this travesty?

How can you fight back when this negativity is directed at you?

Can you build a shield of goodness around your person

That can't be breached, no matter the evil intentions,

A shield that cocoons us from the evil of the world?

Build that cocoon and believe that no one with evil intent will shatter your peace.

A shield built of love, honor, and caring; thus evil will be defeated and goodness restored.

Darkness

The sun is pulled slowly, as if by a magnet, toward its daily destination.

Second by second on the slippery slope, darkness creeps ever nearer.

In that process, however, we are given one of the glories of the day.

The red ball begins to disappear, leaving in its wake rays red flames flowing through the clouds, illuminating the shape and form of everything it touches.

It doesn't last long, but it is breathtaking while it is there.

And then comes the darkness:

The time for renewal;

The time to contemplate;

The time to plan;

The time to be thankful for all we have been given.

Put this time to good use.

Refresh your body and soul so that you will be ready and willing to accept the challenges of tomorrow.

Decision

I have a choice to make.

My mind is blank; I cannot think.

The choice is hard, Lord. I cannot say.

The roads are wide. Which way do I go?

I have commitments; I made them myself.

Why can't you whisper in my ear, "The left road is the way to go."

But I know, Lord, the choice is mine. In your love, you made it so.

Just promise me, Lord, you will always shape my way.

Whatever I do, wherever I go,

If you are with me, the road is mine.

Dinner

When I was small and learning to live,

I sat with my mother and father to eat.

I learned my manners and listened to them talk. I spoke when asked and shared my thoughts.

How life has changed. How busy we've become.

Have we sacrificed a part of our lives?

Can we take the time to honor our parents?

Can we take the time to honor our children and our friends?

Can we sit at the table and enjoy our meals.

Can we sit at the table and share our lives, tell our stories of the day we've lived?

Encourage each other through thick and thin.

Build a bond to help us live through the boundaries of our present world.

A family meal.

Doors to Life

How often the doors of life are shut to our dreams

Uncomprehendingly, we struggle to beat upon that door, not knowing another way to go.

We collapse at the doorstep.

And yet, unknowingly to us, other doors stretch forward.

Can we put wings to our feet and faith in our hearts to step forward, grasp the handle, and enter through the door?

Our dreams are shattered, our spirits humbled, our hearts lying raw battered by the elements—yet we move forward.

Our lives are built upon this rubble,

The doors lying broken and smashed,

No more a purpose to their form.

We climb over the lost dreams, sorrows, and disappointments, and we journey on.

Dream

It was there, shimmering on the horizon: my dream, my goal, the achievement I desired.

What was holding me back?

Why couldn't I move forward?

I knew in my heart: because I was afraid.

Was I foolish to dream? Was I afraid to fail?

What would happen? I'd lose money; my pride would suffer; I would have wasted time.

All good reasons for staying safe!

And yet it wouldn't go away, that dream of mine.

I was standing on the edge of the precipice. Do I fly or stay secure?

My chance was before me. What did I do?

I chose to fly! I rise to the challenge. for this is my time to fill my dream.

Echoes in the Night

I woke from my sleep to the sound of the train whistle.

It flows across the ground like the waves of the ocean.

One, two, three—one soulful call after another!

It matches the cries in my heart.

Could I move forward like the train,

My destination determined with stops along the way,

No deviation or time schedule to be kept?

Could my life be led that way?

Would I want to follow that track?

Do I want to be a sorrowful echo in the night?

Give me the courage to go forward.

Let me decide where I go and what I hope to accomplish.

Let me be a bell that tolls not in sorrow but in joy;

A voice that sings; a heart that laughs and leaves no room for echoes in the night!

Empathy

Can I feel your pain?

Can I know that your heart is breaking into a million little pieces?

Can I know what mental and physical stress you are experiencing?

I can listen; I can sympathize; I can understand what you say.

But can I say that I have known the same?

Unless I have, I cannot say.

But does that mean I shouldn't care?

Does that mean I shouldn't try?

Does that mean my shoulder is not there to cry upon?

Absolutely not!

Let me be the one who cares.

Let me be the one who listens to your woes.

Let me be the one to give you hope when none can be seen.

I will help you manage your grief.

I will help to set you upon your path.

For empathy means loving;

Empathy means wanting to share another's pain;

Empathy means giving of yourself when the opportunity occurs.

Let me be open to the trials and tribulations of others,

Caring always for another human being!

Faces

People walk along. I look at their faces.

Some are serenely beautiful with perfectness stamped on their features;

Others are lined and craggy, full of worry and woe.

And then there are the young, full of hope and anticipation for the day.

And yet, all of these faces hold secrets, sorrows, untold problems behind the mask.

I smile, and they smile—a flash of recognition beyond the obvious.

A knowledge that we share without even speaking!

A quick connection that shares the joy of the day!

Keep us ready and willing for the chances that come our way.

Your smile might be the one that lasts all day.

Façade

What's behind the face? Do we know the person, or is all hidden

Behind the mask that is meant to be seen?

Is it the true spirit, or a false impression hiding the scars of heartbreak and pain?

Is it easier to hide than to conquer the trouble?

Easier to pretend that all is well, that nothing is wrong?

Easier to smile and laugh and pretend joy, than dig deep within?

Courage has left me, pushed deeper and deeper with each passing day.

Can I forget and live forever, never acknowledging that which I have buried?

I have tried–believe me, I have.

But somehow, I know this cannot be!

I have tried to bring forth the burden I carry and wash myself clean.

To forgive my soul and begin anew.

For I know I have been forgiven.

Give me the courage more than I've ever known,

For I will succeed and begin again!

A clean slate to start anew and make my life what it was meant to be!

Feelings

Are you ruled by your feelings, by your flesh?

Do you allow your feelings to have free rein in your life?

When you wish to do something, do you stop to consider whether it is wise,

Or do you react to your desire without conscious thought?

Do you give in to temper, to indulgent behavior, to un-healthy actions without thought?

If we could stop and consider our actions, would we react in the same manner,

Or would we reconsider and decide that the actions we are contemplating would not be in our best interests?

Strengthen your spirit by denying those feelings that challenge you every day.

As you grow stronger, your spirit will rule over your feelings.

You and your spirit will be in control, not your feelings.

Don't wander down the path with no control, no purpose.

Live the life that God has planned for you.

Forgiveness

Forgiveness is the window to your soul,

Glowing as rays of light bounce against its reflection,

Nourished with warmth by your deed.

Or it is dull and streaked,

Mired with dirt and grime blocking all sustenance.

The soul is thus left with an insidious collection of iniquities

That compound until blackness obscures its sight.

The opportunity lies at our feet, quietly waiting for us to bend down and feel its weight.

Heavy—undoubtedly so.

Impossible, no, for cleansing requires diligence,

And diligence lies in our heart for us to use.

Forgotten

I did it today, Lord. I let down a friend.

Completely forgotten was the date we had made.

She anticipated and hoped, and I in my busyness remembered not.

Just when I think I am growing in grace,

I slip and fall flat upon my face.

She forgave—to her glory, not mine.

You forgave—to your glory for all time.

Good Deeds

How do you live your life, my friend?

Do you expect thanks for everything you do?

Is your giving conditioned upon a response, building up goodness against a need?

Frustrated anger wells in your heart against those who ignore your deeds.

Do you decide that you will withhold your help because of this lack of appreciation?

Is this what giving is all about?

Or is giving done with a pure heart,

Expecting no reward, no response, no acclimation of your good deeds?

That is the true meaning of giving:

The wonderful warm feeling in your heart that says,

"I did a good deed today."

Happiness

Can you define the meaning of this word?

Can you categorize all that this encompasses?

Have you given any thought to what gives you happiness?

Does it take a tremendous occurrence to bring you joy,

Or do you appreciate and enjoy the small things in life that can take place?

The smile of a friend; the love of your family; the beauty of nature; the kindness of a stranger, the thankfulness of good health.

Is it possible that these daily memories that we take for granted may bring you happiness?

Give it a thought;

Give it a chance.

Appreciate the little things, and you will find the only true path of a happy life.

He Died to Set Me Free

Because I was weak, he gave me his strength.

Because I was selfish, he showed me how to give.

Because I was fearful, he showed me the worst fear of all.

Because I was uncaring, he showed me how to pause and reflect.

Because I was drifting aimlessly alone, tied to the cares of this world, he gave me a new direction.

Because I was sure I was right, he gently showed me otherwise.

Because of his love, he died to sct me free.

Insight

Insight is the ability to see the situation clearly and correctly.

Do you have this ability, and if you do not, do you seek the wisdom needed?

Or do you forge ahead, wanting no counsel or wisdom, your own mind selecting the path that you will tread?

What of your decisions? Have they been wise, bringing success to all your endeavors?

Or do you find yourself digging a deeper hole each and every time?

Do you intend to let the hole get so deep that it collapses onto itself,

So deep that it eradicates the path of escape,

So deep that no matter how you struggle, you can't see the light?

Is this what you have planned for your life?

Stop now and change your path.

Open your mind and ask for help.

Seek advice and study the facts.

It's there for you, the knowledge you need.

There is no guarantee that you will be wise,

No guarantee that you will be successful,

But you will know that you gave it your best,

And that is the greatest gift of all.

Learning

Early in life, we begin our journey;

The road to knowledge lies ahead.

Through stages of milestones,

We learn by living, we learn my doing;

We learn by listening, we learn by reading;

We learn from others, and we learn by ourselves.

Every day is a new experience.

We are little sponges floating in the ocean, absorbing all and expelling none.

Do we have room for all we learn? Apparently so.

Some are captured by the lure of learning; to others, their paths lead to learning by doing.

Whichever way it comes to us, it never ends, this love of discovery.

How blessed we are for the gift we are given.

Listening

I hear your voice as the words tumble out;

They hang in the air as birds on the wing.

My emotions arise, a wall blocking my sight.

I can't respond, boxed in by my feelings, unable to hear.

I miss the chance to linger there.

Beneath your words lie meanings unknown.

Were I to know, perhaps I could bear the secret fears locked in your heart.

The traits from generations before!

The pain of suffering from whence you came!

Oh, teach me to listen with my head as well as my heart

That I might learn the meaning of listening.

Memories

Miss you, oh how I do.

Each passing day, remembrances steal into my heart:

A fellow friend, a time of year, a physical likeness, a song that I hear.

Each occurrence brings back to me the wonderful memories that linger in my heart.

They won't go away. I won't allow them to.

I won't dwell on what I don't have, but I will cherish and feel warmth from the happiness that I felt.

I have moved on,

Accepted what I cannot change.

But life is built on small pebbles accumulating day after day,

Stretching upward toward the sky, a huge monument to the life I lead.

Some are black: the unhappy, the mistakes, the losses.

Some are white representing joy: my family, my life success, and the wonderful people I have met.

But a huge part of that life was the people I loved and lost.

Always and forever with me!

Wendy Brooks

Mistake

Have you made a mistake?

Do you feel really stupid?

Do you regret your actions but have no way to rectify the situation?

No way to say, "I was stupid, and I apologize"?

Do you punish yourself endlessly?

Why is it so hard to forgive ourselves?

Why do we allow the mistake to rule our lives?

Rather, can we take the steps to allow peace to dwell,

To know that we didn't mean to cause any pain?

Can we forgive ourselves and determine that we have learned a lesson,

And can we strive to never make the same mistake again?

It is only through mistakes that we mature and grow strong enough to live a mistakeless life.

Morning

I hear the birds calling their greetings of good morning.

Through rain, through shine, they are there to awaken us with a smile—

One of God's many gifts given freely to us.

Do we notice? Do we care?

Can we find the beauty in these gifts?

We can't earn them, can't buy them, can't design or build them.

They are part of the wonderful thing called nature.

The sun, the moon, the rainbow, the stars—the list is endless.

Happiness will be yours if you stop to count these blessings each and every day.

Don't be so busy, in such a hurry, rushing here and there,

Wearing blindfolds to everything but what you feel you have to do.

Take a few minutes every day to enjoy the panorama that is nature.

Motivation

What motivates us?

What gives us the push to accomplish all that lies before us?

Does motivation come easily to you, or is it much easier to ignore all and slip into the world of leisure?

Leisure drains all desire for accomplishment.

Leisure saps our strength and makes us unable to achieve anything.

Can you find an example?

Someone you admire;

Someone who lives a life of purpose and meaning;

Someone who succeeds when success doesn't seem possible;

Someone who has succeeded and failed and succeeded again.

Study that life and learn what you can.

Take what this lesson teaches you and incorporate it into your life.

Large or small deeds—they are all the same.

It is the motivation to accomplish that is the important goal.

Make your life on earth a worthwhile life.

Mountains

Majestic mountains, your peaks roll on, sister to the ocean's waves,

Impervious to the onslaught of today,

Living as a thousand years ago and as you will a thousand years hence.

Roads have been carved relentlessly out of your landscape.

Civilization pounds hour by hour upon your backs.

All these have not significantly eroded your beauty.

Trees line your slopes, layer upon layer, reaching majestically to the sun.

Beneath their branches, they shelter the fauna of the forest.

The exquisite beauty of a delicate wild flower;

The intricate form of the fern;

The moss tenaciously clinging wherever it can.

Among all this, the animals find their home.

Small or large, they find the perfect environment for themselves,

Tucked away among the shadows of the glen.

Forests of the primeval, forests of the future, they stand.

Majestic monuments of truth and love!

My Garden

How can I explain what my garden means to me?

It is a worth beyond words.

It is a gift, a blessing for my soul.

God has given us nature to enjoy.

No charge, no obligation, no sacrifice,

Just a pleasure to sooth our path.

A time to spend with nature:

Smelling the fresh air, listening to the birds sing,

Digging in the dirt, watching the birth of an idea!

Forgetting, for a space in time, all the trials and tribulations that life brings,

Cleansing the mind of all issues except those that the garden deems necessary.

What will I plant this year?

What will the color scheme be?

Shall I make new beds, and how will they be designed?

It is a mind-boggling task, but oh, what pleasure it does bring.

If you have never availed yourself of gardening, give it a try.

It's not easy; it's hard work—but joyful beyond words.

Nature

Trees standing silhouetted against the white snow, candles upon the hill.

The blue sky forms a backdrop while the cows wander over the slopes.

A still life of yesterday, today, or tomorrow!

Nature is the constant rejuvenating force in our lives,

Accessible to all but often ignored.

Drink it into your senses; allow it to fill your soul; relax in its peace.

The soothing balm for a busy world.

Obstacles

What obstacles are placed on our path??

Are they small obstacles easily moved aside,

Or great mountains looming before us?

Maybe for us, it's a mixture of all.

Do we really believe that our lives will be obstacle free,

And we will merrily zoom through life like a butterfly, gracefully flitting from flower to flower?

Do we give it much thought this flight of ours, and would it matter if we did?

Anticipating bad or good in our lives is pure conjecture,

However believing in the positive is the path to contentment.

The obstacle looms up. How do we handle it?

Do we shrink back and become the turtle in its shell, afraid to face that which has to be addressed?

Do we bury it deep, try to live as though it wasn't there, hoping it will solve itself?

Or do we find the courage to seek help from friends, family, and professionals who can help us navigate the obstacles in our way?

The choice is ours.

One Light

One light I see, far down a long black corridor.

The walls are damp and clammy to my touch.

The floor is penetratingly cold to my bare feet.

The air is foul with the stench of mold and decay.

I am afraid, yet the light calls to me.

I feel the light is my hope;

It calls me to warmth, to a love never ending,

To a love that endures no matter what.

It does not flicker or grow dim; it stays steady.

Keep straight, feet; do not stumble or slip, for the light will be mine.

Let no obstacle fall in my path, for I will not be stopped.

I alone can clear the way.

The corridor looks long now.

It will grow shorter, and the light will not fade.

Keep my eyes ever on the light at the end.

Wendy Brooks

One Lily

The will to live is a lily growing in a field.

At the beginning, the shoot is hidden in the dark brown earth.

Encased in a warm cocoon, nurtured by the elements,

It pushes upward unswervingly erect toward its purpose.

Countless enemies thwart this growth.

Nature that sustains life also sends the destroyers:

The buffeting winds, relentless drought,

Searing rays of the sun that beat down, feet that carelessly tread.

Some fall by the wayside, unable to combat the trials.

More beautiful is the lily that reaches its apex.

More perfect because of adversity.

One perfect lily!

Maybe not symmetrical in form or size,

Leaves drooping in the restless breeze,

Petals bearing the scars of ragged edges.

Perfect because it stands a monument to its struggle!

Nature and Mankind.

A testimony to survival.

One Star

A star came to live in my life.

It shone brightly with little chance for dimness to come upon itself.

Then the light went out in my horizon, leaving me duller than before.

But as I look upon heaven, I see that star shining as brightly as before.

And when my maker says it's time,

I will ascend to my position beside that star,

To shine brightly forever more.

Pain

As I lay here, pain is my constant companion.

Months have passed with endless hours of nothingness.

People come and go, yet I feel no encouragement.

Sliding, sliding, yet faster I go.

No spark within to flame anew; I'm quenching its power with the waves of hopelessness.

Stranger, do you care for me?

One word to light a spark! If only one could care.

Dare I dream that you might be that light for me?

Peace

I took a walk through the autumn calm,

The weeds so tall they formed a wall.

The grass-crushed pathway held hollows waiting to prey upon my unwary feet.

The crickets jumped with each step I took—a road to be covered, a little brook.

I sat and listened and looked.

I was the reflection;

I was the sky.

I danced over rocks,

I swept through the trees.

I found the calm that nourished my soul.

I found the peace that nature provides.

Take the time to find that path,

For it is your responsibility to guard your soul.

Perfect Soul

A perfect soul will find the pure and therein dwell through the ages.

The purity of a child unsullied by the world.

The purity of nature, the field of daffodils swaying in the breeze.

The setting sun ablaze with color, the miracle of new growth each spring.

Absorb the pure; drink it into your being.

Ugliness is there, we understand, but the reality is not a force that has been won by sinking into the inhumanities.

Think pure and deal with evil. In this way, your soul will fly above the mire,

Enabling you to bring purity to the fore.

Procrastination

Do we choose not to do the details that need to be done?

We say, "I'll do it next week when I have the time.

I'll take care of it, when I feel the need.

There are more important problems to tax my mind."

Do we realize that we load our minds with all the small details that never get done?

They pile one on top of another,

Until the pile overwhelms us and leaves us unable to do anything.

It makes us worry and fret every day, and it changes our attitudes to life.

Instead, let us take one task a week,

Decide on a solution, put it into action,

And cross it off our list.

Our pile will get smaller, never totally eliminated,

But consistently tackling the issues that we must address.

We will feel the pride of accomplishment,

Feel the satisfaction of achievement,

Feel the easing of our stress.

Make your road in life the way it was meant to be.

Rain

It's cloudy today; the sun hides behind the clouds.

The sky is grey, not the shinning blue we so love.

All of the clouds are full of water, just waiting to open and empty upon our earth.

Not as beautiful as a blue sky day, but beautiful in its own way.

Do we need the rain?

Absolutely: it nourishes the soil, giving life to the dry ground.

The forests absorb the rain and sing in happiness.

The animals of the forest drink the water that lies on the fauna and give thanks for the moisture that satisfies their needs.

The trees absorb and continue to grow, reaching upward to the sky.

Without this life-giving moisture, our land would dry,

Our forests would die, our flowers would be no more.

Our land as we know it would be lost.

So let us celebrate this cloudy day,

And hope that the clouds will bless us with their life-giving gift.

Repetition

How much of our lives are a repetition of seconds flowing before?

As I sit in this place, I am reminded of those other times.

Memories fly across my mind in profusion:

Memories of you, more profound because there are no new memories to be formed.

How meaningful repetitions become when life is lost.

Each simple duty, thought, or word, becomes a symphony.

Color blares at the senses;

Nature is a moving, throbbing sculpture;

Love is not just a word; it permeates your soul and rushes through your dispensable body.

Feel the preciousness of repetition.

Taste the tang that it offers you.

Flee not from its duty, for through it lies your life.

Sharing

My heart was sore with pain,

My mind torn apart with questions,

When you, a stranger, walked into my life.

You shared your hurts with me, unburdened your soul.

Your willingness to share comforted me.

And after some time, I was able to let my hurt escape.

I, who had talked to few.

I, who hid all my secrets behind a façade.

Because of you, my load was lighter.

Your loving heart obeyed, your gentle spirit cried,

And I found strength for the journey ahead.

Silence

What does silence mean to you?

Is it a fear that lodges in your heart, or is it peace and calm that strengthens your soul?

Oftentimes these feelings are influenced by circumstances beyond our control.

Does it mean that we have to follow that path,

That no changes can be made in the way we live?

We have the choice; we have the control.

Do not live with the old ways.

If silence is a fear for you, take it out and analyze.

Can you put a reason to the fear,

Or is it completely out of your comprehension, nagging at your memory but lying just out of reach?

Can you put it to rest and use the gift of silence?

Silence is a valuable commodity:

It enables us to keep a balance in our lives.

It rests our bodies and our souls.

It allows us to keep up with the pace of daily living.

Our lives are full of communication;

Everywhere we turn, we are battered with information.

We carry this with us daily.

Nowhere can we escape the technology of our times.

Nowhere can we turn off the flood.

Our brains are overloaded each and every day.

Therefore, we need our secret place;

The place of quiet, calm, and serenity;

The place of contemplation and renewal.

Don't deprive your body of this benefit.

Give yourself the gift of silence.

Sky

The endless sky stretches around us;

Its moods encompass our feelings:

The blue of tranquility and love;

The peace of a soul in quiet repose;

The happiness of a child at play.

Oh, child, I wish you blue.

The black of the angry storm:

Power beyond our thoughts;

Exhilarating force moving across the heavens;

Fear and awe for the things that we know not.

Sunset—oh, beauty beyond comprehension;

Vibrant and alive, you flash across the horizon.

I gaze and am astounded at your perfection.

I am thrown to my knees in humility.

Sunrise—eternal hope! A new sky stretching before you!

Move forward, knowing not what's ahead,

But always pressing on to your final sky.

Solitude

When I am alone, my soul reaches to my father.

He touches my spirit and rejuvenates my faith.

I am his to use.

Cease your struggling, your willfulness; listen to your soul.

He cannot speak to you, my friend, while you struggle.

He cannot speak to you while you direct your thoughts.

Be still and reflect on his wonders:

The power of the wind; the glory of the sky;

The majesty of a mountain, the strength of a tree!

His presence is around you. Can you not see?

Love from a friend who comforts us in sorrow;

Help from a stranger who ministers in sickness;

The touch of a loved one—

His presence is around you. Can you not see?

Be still and feel his love.

Sorrow

I swirl in a cloud of darkness, its turbulence holding me clutched in its power.

I can't break away; I push against the power, but it holds me in.

The sorrow is so powerful, I can hardly breathe.

I try to rationalize, but nothing makes sense.

I feel as though I were in a coma, breathing but nothing else.

Suddenly the cloud is pierced by a shaft of light.

The beam aims downward, settling on three figures.

Why does it illuminate them?

What are they to do with me?

And then as I regain my senses, I know.

My children, whom God has given me to love.

My children, whom God has entrusted to my care.

My responsibility for their upbringing and happiness.

A purpose through my sorrow!

Give me strength, oh Lord, to handle my grief.

Courage to be the person I should.

Your love has always been with me and will be evermore,

Love never ending.

Soulmate

Side by side, we stroll along, my partner and I.

Some would say, "How lucky you are that you have found the perfect one."

And I would say, "How right you are." for there is only one.

I searched and searched to no avail.

I thought I would not be blessed at all.

Then you came quite by accident, and I knew that it was you:

The one who makes me complete.

The one who makes my faults bearable.

The one who makes my strength even stronger.

And lucky for me, I recognized that which had to be.

I knew that you were the partner for me.

So as we tackle life's difficulties, life's challenges, life's rewards,

We do it together, cherishing each and every memory as they occur.

The pathway of life is not necessarily lighter,

But easier because I have you by my side:

Someone to share with, someone to cry with, someone to find joy with.

And so I say, thank you, God, for bringing me my soulmate

So that together we can make a difference in each and every day.

Stairway to Heaven

Steps stretching before me, waiting for my footsteps.

Behind they lie, silently mastered by me.

Pain, laughter, sadness, and joy scattered over the stairway.

I turn and look, a moment's pause;

Savor but do not dwell, least I tumble backward.

Forward each day, step by step I go,

Sometimes steady, other times haltingly,

Keeping my soul aligned to heaven but my eyes attuned to the challenges lying before me.

I must not stumble on a hurting heart, overlook a crying need, or step upon a fallen soul.

Forward each day until the door I see opening wide to me—the doorway to my home.

Stillness

Can you picture a lake, smooth as glass,

Trees standing perfectly still, no birds flying from tree to tree,

No noise from small animals scurrying in the leaves, no insects darting among the fauna,

Nothing but perfect stillness?

And I, sitting on the bank, scarcely breathing,

Not wanting to disturb this beautiful stillness.

Could this ever be?

Yes, but rarely in the world we live in.

The perfect space is in ourselves.

It is there, waiting for us when the need is overwhelming.

It gives us time to completely let go,

Allows our spirit to fly and soar,

Washes our bodies free of stress and strain.

Our perfect space rejuvenates our spirit,

Enabling us to tackle all the joy and stress that encompasses our daily lives.

Keep that sweet spot handy and picture the peace and tranquility.

It is the lifeline to our sanity and happiness.

Strength

The greatest strength is the strength to be weak.

Know when to abdicate,

When to submit to the absolute good of another without thoughts of reward.

The pain might be acute, the dreams might be shattered,

But weakness in such times reaps its own consolation—

Not in terms of this world, but in the ultimate goodness of the next.

So be not afraid to lose that identity.

Be strong enough to be weak.

Stubbornness

What is this trait?

Stubbornness or determination—what difference can there be?

How do we define the meaning of the word?

If I have a goal that I have to fulfill,

Is that stubbornness or determination?

If I have a desire from deep in my heart,

Is that stubbornness or determination?

If I see a problem that I am compelled to correct,

Is that stubbornness or determination?

On has a negative connotation, the other positive.

I feel compelled to question this designation.

Stubbornness, when associated with stick-to-itiveness, equates success.

Determination, without checks and balances, can lead to defeat.

So when you use either word to define a soul,

Be mindful and considerate of that definition.

Sunshine

The darkness lies upon the land.

The peace of night encompasses all.

Small rodents quietly move across the ground,

Safely finding food before the start of dawn.

Slowly the sun moves across the horizon, the light deepening second by second.

The sun beginning as a dot, growing and growing

Until we see the round ball it is meant to be.

Beams of sunlight flash to the ground,

Warming and nourishing all below with their life-sustaining force.

Flowers needing the beams to fully open their petals;

Trees absorbing the beams to burst forth with leaves;

Grass receiving the light that turns it green.

Humans exposing our skin to the warmth,

Exposing our hearts to the joy,

To the happiness that we feel as we gaze at the sun.

There is nothing quite like the sun,

Nothing that gives us such joy

And gives us food for our souls and bodies.

Even on days when the sun may be hidden, we know that it is there, doing the job it was given to do.

Thank You

What a little word this is, but what a powerful message it sends.

The emotions that it draws are all encompassing and have no competition.

What would the world be like if no one ever said thank you?

If you did a kind act, and the person just looked at you with a blank face?

If you asked a favor, it was given, and the response was nothing?

Although sometimes I believe we say it without thought,

It is better than not saying it at all.

Consideration, caring, and kindness are combined in this small word.

It makes us better people to voice these words.

It makes us want to smile.

The Forest

A highway blasted through the middle of the forest,

Sheer rock that has yielded to the demand.

Trees for miles and miles in towering hills,

Rounded perfectly in shades of green.

How many trees does this forest hold?

Could we count the number? Is it impossible to do?

The setting sun illuminates the peaks and angles,

Forming a backdrop for the clouds;

It is here for us to enjoy,

Here for us to appreciate,

To take a moment to wonder at the miracle that we see.

Not man-made but nature at its best.

Let's indulge our senses on this ride through a beautiful forest

And say thanks to God for another gift he has bestowed on us.

The Hospital

The hospital where our greatest dream—

And your most feared nightmare can occur.

Where research, medicine, and scientific knowledge are practiced.

Where people who care for people choose to work.

Where making us whole and well is everyone's goal.

Although it is not where any of us plan to be,

It is where we have to be when health obstacles arise.

What is our role to play in this scenario?

We can't make diagnosis,

We can't administer the medicine,

We can't perform the operation.

But we can strive to think positively.

Have an attitude that says, "I will overcome."

The mind is a marvelous part of our body,

Influencing us always in the direction we instruct.

So use your mind in a worthwhile way.

Help the hospital staff accomplish their goals and make you whole again.

A team working together bringing about miracles!

Wendy Brooks

The Moon

I was driving today in the early morn,

When I glanced to the right and saw the moon,

A large white oval glowing so bright.

I thought to myself as I gloried in the sight,

"What gifts we've been given to lighten our way."

Then I thought of other wonders that grace my vision.

The sun so round, sparkling bright in the sky with beams of warmth.

The trees so straight with branches stretched forward; in winter so bare, in summer so bright.

The flowers that bloom, the colors so glorious,

The rivers that flow through hill and through dale.

How can we be struggling with sorrow and depression?

God has given us so much at no cost to us.

We have the means to find joy in every day.

Do you grab it or throw it away?

The choice is yours so take it today.

The Rock

Thank you, God, for being the rock that steadies me in this whirling sea that is our world,

For being the rock that holds me up when all around me starts to crumble.! Thank you, God, for cradling me against your gift when I begin to doubt,

For the peace I feel as I lean against the rock and feel the sun breaking into my soul.

This endearing and steady rock nudges me forward toward my path when I am reluctant to move.

The rock will stand forever.

Nothing will move it away from my side because you have promised me this gift.

How I pray that others will find the rock and bask in its glory.

The Sand

Countless feet have trod upon your back.

The sea sweeps and encroaches towards your beginnings.

You have been blown and eroded from your home,

And yet you are inexhaustible.

You are a haven in your warmth, a joy in your texture, a beauty in your solitude.

I observe your expanse, and I am fortified.

The Sea

Vibrations of power flow through your waves as they pound against the shore.

Tumbling and churning, they sweep, forcing everything to obey.

In your depths, the ages have lived, oblivious to the forces far above,

Sheltering and providing sustenance for all your inhabitants.

At times, a calmness belies your power;

A stillness lies across your expanse.

The sky caresses you with color and mirrors its beauty, and peace reigns.

Eternity has used your fruits, finding gratification for tangible and intangible needs.

You have been faithful, never refusing to extend the lifeline that you hold,

Although requiring, at times, that man stretch his capacity to its fullness.

Endlessly you sweep, giving us your fruits for our edification, always and forever.

Wendy Brooks

The Seed

The seed, brown and shriveled—of what use can you be?

Have you beauty, or purpose, or need?

Are you thrown by the wayside for want of value?

And yet if someone cares, if someone sees a value in your shrunken shape,

She will place you in the warmth of a cocoon,

And there, a metamorphosis will occur.

Nature's love will shower you until you burst forth.

All the beauty and purpose inherent in your being

Is now released for all to see.

Do you recognize the shriveled seed,

Or do you pass it by for the obvious, thereby missing the opportunity to see what might be?

The Son

Can you comprehend the sacrifice of a son?

To knowingly send him to hardships, untold pain, and sorrow?

To remove him from peace and place him in toil?

To request of him to save mankind, whatever the cost might be?

To understand that many would not listen—and indeed, many would scoff and laugh?

How great a love for man!

I have received this sacrifice.

Do I respond in kind?

The Trip

You took a trip, three friends of old,

Explored the west, and had a blast.

Told stories, jokes galore,

Reminisced for hours, had political debates,

Rested only when needed.

Memories forever,

Never to be replaced.

Part of the legacy that is life!

Time

A capsule of judgment is a second of time;

It escapes us without our knowledge.

Nothing worthwhile accomplished.

No good or kind deed done.

No soft word of love spoken,

No smile bestowed upon another.

No helping hand offered or sympathy extended.

No compassion or tear for mankind.

How many seconds will you have?

Life is a fragile cobweb, entwined around your soul.

Tenaciously it clings until a storm blows it away,

And the soul stands bare a second, for dissolution of a cobweb.

Man's seconds are capable of untold greatness.

The capacity is unending and eternal.

Behind us, they are lost;

Before us, they stretch, pulsating with hope.

Grab your seconds and make them count.

To My Mother

I stand here in the middle of my life and look at you,

Not as a child to a mother image, but rather in introspection.

I see a life full of giving without thought of yourself.

I see a life deemed worthy of emulating.

I see faith permeating your being.

I see hope always shining through sickness, pain, and sorrow.

I see charity a living workable ideal.

Through all, I see beyond to the one perfect one who made you, my mother.

Today

As I awoke today, I asked myself,

"What chance might come my way?"

Would I see a face with sorrowful eyes?

Would I hear a voice choked with tears?

Could I respond with a tender word an arm around a friend?

Or would I turn my back and miss my chance to give some peace?

Could I be brave enough to show you love

Although I might be shunned?

Give me strength, Lord, that I might be the person that you envision of me.

Give me the knowledge to speak or keep my peace.

Above all, let me show the love that helps us succeed.

Trees

How brown and bare you stand, silhouetted against the blue sky.

Some of you are straight, each branch perfectly spaced in symmetrical unity.

Others are gnarled and misshapen, bent from the pounding of the winds.

Yet under each of you is the life ready to burst through,

The skin becoming lavish in form and color,

The spectacle of rebirth.

A poetry in motion set before our eyes in continuous succession.

We count on this rebirth; we expect it to happen every year without fail.

Care we for the miracle before us?

Dare we study the significance?

Bare we the soul that understands?

Unhappiness

What brings us unhappiness?

Is it the world that encompasses us, or is it the world that lives within us?

Do we handle the stresses that occur, or do we absorb them without resolve?

Do we build mountains out of issues, or do we put them in their place according to seriousness?

How we handle these problems is the secret to our happiness or our unhappiness.

If we are given a life-threatening illness, a marital breakup, a financial setback,

Do we collapse and let the tide of conflict carry us away?

Or do we find the courage to challenge the outcome,

To fight the situation rather than letting the situation fight us?

Do we let little issues bother us unnecessarily,

Or do we put them in their box and bury them once and for all?

We have the power. We have the control.

It's what we do with it that tells the tale.

So let's make our lives as happy as we can.

Every minute is a gift—let's not waste a second.

Vacation

Put away for a time the chaotic lifestyle, decisions, obligations, and necessities.

You have the time to rest the mind; turn off the machine and let it recharge.

No crises to solve, no deadlines to meet, no reports to write, no customers to charm.

You have the time to rest the body. Arise when you wish, go to bed at dawn.

Eat snacks all day, or don't eat at all. Exercise all day or lie in the sun.

Explore new places, or visit familiar ones. Visit a spa, ride the rapids, go country hopping, or stay at home.

The choice is yours.

No wonder we love vacations. They are our yearly dream.

We plan and look forward to those times we have coming. The memories we make are ours forever.

So here's to our vacations, whatever or wherever they may be.

Waiting

It seems my life is anchored in waiting.

Each day something new occurs that necessitates my patience.

If I were queen, my subjects would immediately respond.

But since I'm not, I'm always waiting.

Minutes, hours—the time is never set in my favor, it seems, only in the unpredictability of solution.

My patience is at an end. Why me?

Why should I experience this difficulty?

Am I the only one to experience this pain?

Is there a lesson to learn?

Would I be happier if I could wait?

Would my path be smoother without impatience?

Can I have the courage to try?

Waiting—An Act of Will

Waiting.

Much of life finds us lingering so impatiently, annoyingly aggravated within.

Seconds and minutes wasted in useless emotions.

How do we utilize this precious allotment?

Minutes turn into hours of discontent.

Rubbing shoulders with others who incur our wrath.

The circle ever widens.

Our thoughtless words weave a spiderweb over all who enter.

Rather, use that second for introspection—

A capability available but seldom employed.

Use that second for thankfulness—

A quality commonly overlooked.

Use that second for forgiveness—

A purpose bringing peace of mind.

Waiting—a significant act of will by any who find the way!

Printed in the United States
By Bookmasters